Plátanos en Nuestro Patio

Copyright © 2023 by Ro Peña
Published by Stirred Stories.

All rights reserved.

No part of this publication may be reproduced, distributed, or transmitted in any form or by any means, including photocopying, recording, or other electronic or mechanical methods, without the prior written permission of the publisher, except as permitted by U.S. copyright law. For permission requests, contact hello@stirredstories.com.

First edition: September 2023

ATTENTION SCHOOLS AND BUSINESSES:
Stirred Stories books are available at a discount for bulk purchase. For more information, please email sales@stirredstories.com.

Plátanos en Nuestro Patio

Written by: Ro Peña

Illustrated by: Lillie DeLecuona

To my ancestors who live through me and guide me with unwavering love.

There are plátanos en nuestro patio.

Bunches of green plantains, like hopeful fingers reaching up to touch the clear blue sky. These bunches grow on stalwart plátano trees that are as tall as me, times three. Their leaves are big and wide, like the waving fans I see on Sundays en la iglesia.

I hear Abuela calling.
"¡Corazón, despierta! It's time!"

"¡Voy, Abuela! I'll be right there!"
I rub the sleep from my eyes, hop out of
bed and shuffle my feet into my chancletas.

Abuela doesn't like when I walk around the house descalza. She worries I'll catch a cold.

But I always remind her that as long as there's vaporú in the house, I'll be ok!

"Bendición, Abuela."
"Dios te bendiga, Corazón."

She cradles my cheeks in her worshiping hands and looks lovingly into my eyes, holding me between her palms like a cherished artifact. I'm proof that our ancestors still exist within us.

MWAHH!

Me Next!

Abuela kisses me on the forehead.

She smells of sofrito: the seasoning she uses on all of her most delicious dishes. The scent of fresh garlic and onions mixed with peppers and cilantro. Pero más que nada, she smells of unconditional love.

"Corazón, it's time to cut the tree down and harvest el racimo de plátanos."

Plátanos are green and tough — like the Hulk. Except, plátanos are patient, too — like Abuela waiting to see her son, my Tío Tomás, again.

"Abuela, can't we just cut the bunch off and leave the tree so it can grow more plátanos? I don't want the tree to die."

"You're so thoughtful, Corazón. Pero, no. Lo siento. When the bunch of green plantains is done growing, the tree does not fruit again and it will die. Es el ciclo de la vida."

"But it took sooo long to grow. Almost two whole years!

I remember because Gordo had just been born when we planted it, and now he's this big!"

So BIG!

"Sí. You're right. This mata de plátano did take some time to grow, ¡pero, mira! It's provided us with this beautiful racimo. And now, when we cut it down, there will be room for other plátano trees to grow and provide us with even more plátanos. Generation after generation. Así es la vida. ¿Entiendes?"

"Yeah, I understand."

My abuela is an Indigenous warrior.

Her eyes, fitted with the wisdom of our ancestors, are instinctual and determined. Her arms are strong and black, like her morning cafecito.

She wields her machete in her right hand, gripping to it like one holds on to oral stories. La historia de su gente. An extension of herself.

"Vamos a darle las gracias. It's important that we thank this tree for what it has given us. For the connection to our roots. Our land. Our people. For nourishing our bodies. And for teaching us paciencia."

Thank you...

Abuela has always taught me to give thanks. To the plants and animals we encounter. To the people we learn from. To the earth and the sky. To the beginning and ending of a day. To patience. And to myself, for being myself.

Abuela cuts the bunch off from the felled tree and gives me a warning: "Corazón, remember, when you are picking up the plátanos, try not to get tree sap on you. It stains."

"Ok, Abuela!"

I carefully pick up the bunch. It's heavy and awkward to hold. Like the first time I held my baby brother.

I take it into the kitchen where Abuela teaches me how to cut each row of the plátanos off.

We have to let the sap from the plátanos drain for an hour before we can do anything with them. I remind myself that the thing about plátanos es que nos enseñan paciencia.

"Abuela, can we have maduros with arro'habichuelaycarne tonight?"
"Paciencia, Corazón. These plátanos won't be ready for maduros tonight."

I know Abuela is right. These plátanos are green. Not the kind of plátanos for sweet maduros. I'll have to wait a few weeks for them to ripen and turn mostly black with some patches of yellow. I can barely wait.

"¿Sabes, Corazón? You're just like your Tío Tomás. He loves maduros too."

"I hope we can eat maduros together again soon."

"Me too. Pero hay que tener..."

"Paciencia."

"Abuela, with all these plátanos we can probably make about a thousand pieces of maduros, right?"

"Ay, Corazón, siempre comiendo con los ojos. We can't possibly eat these all ourselves!

Not all of these plátanos are destined to be maduros. And not all of these plátanos are meant for our bellies."

The phone rings and Abuela answers.

"Aló, dígame."

She holds the phone between her shoulder and her ear. She purses her lips and points with them, motioning for me to pass her the broom. Abuela is always cleaning something.

I can tell it's Doña Rodríguez from the way Abuela smiles and says, "¡Hola, vecina! ¿Cómo estás? We just harvested some plátanos, would you like some?"

Moments later, Doña Rodríguez is standing in our kitchen. She is a short, rosy, brown woman who commands space. Her hair is rolled up in rolos like a head full of colorful candy.

"I'm so glad I called! I was looking out my window earlier and I saw you and Corazón harvesting el racimo de plátanos. I just knew today would be the perfect day to cook mangú con los tres golpes!"

"¿Mangú con los tres golpes? What's that?"
Abuela and Doña Rodríguez exchange a smile.
"¿Me permites?" "¡Claro!"

Doña Rodríguez grabs a plátano and a knife. Holding one in each hand, she cuts both ends of the plátano off. She slides the knife down one of the plátano's edges and guides her thumb down the cut, pulling away the peel. She does the same thing with two other plátanos.

"Y ahora tú, Corazón. Cut the plátanos in half and then cut those halves the long way, too."

She hands me the plátanos and the knife. I do just as she says.

When the plátanos are soft enough to poke a fork in, they are done. Doña Rodríguez drains most of the water. She adds a half-stick of butter and smashes the plátanos with a fork. Abuela passes me a cup of cold water to slowly add into the pot as Doña Rodríguez continues to smash the plátanos.

The mix is soft and smooth. But mostly, it's ready to be eaten!

¡Mangú con los tres golpes!

We talk... mostly bochinche... as we eat our delicious breakfast.

Soon after, Doña Rodríguez says her goodbyes. Abuela hands her some plátanos. She places them in her bag.

"I'm off to see Señora Reyes. I hear she has some aguacate ready to pick from her tree.

Thank you for the plátanos! ¡Adios!"

And as quickly as she came, Doña Rodríguez was out the door.

"Buenos días, Don Martínez."

"¡Hola, Corazón!"

Don Martínez is the color of Boca Chica — a white, sandy beach not too far from our home. His skin is soft and worn like leather. I can barely tell where his mouth is behind his mustache. But I know he's smiling, because he mostly smiles with his eyes.

He sells pasteles en hoja: well-seasoned mashed plátanos, stuffed with ground beef and wrapped in a plátano leaf that's boiled to perfection. A gift full of flavor.

He keeps the pasteles nice and hot in an enormous pot in the back of a cart he pieced together himself. The cart is made of wood and nails attached to an old bike.

I hand Don Martínez the five plátanos. In exchange, he hands me three pasteles en hoja. He unwraps one for me. The steam dances a rhythmic merengue on its way to my nose.

Don Martínez squirts a zig of ketchup and a zag of mayo on my pastel. I can already taste the blend of flavors seconds away from my tongue.

"Gracias, Don Martínez."
"De nada, Corazón."

As fast as Don Martínez came, he was off...

"Pasteles... Pasteles... ¡paaasteeeeleeees!"

This is mi barrio
My community
The rooster crowing en la mañana
People selling food from their carritos

Vecinos calling their children to come inside and eat
"¡Ya está la comida!"

The next day, I hear las ollas banging. Like an alarm clock encouraging me to start my day. Abuela is already busy.

I hear the tap, tap, tapping of rain on the zinc roof.

When I go into the kitchen I see my older cousin Yakelin seated at the table.

"Yakelin!"
"Corazón!"

We hug for so long. Long enough that it almost feels like we've made up for all the time they'd been away. They smell like cocoa butter. Warm and comforting.

Tío Tomás is Yakelin's papi. They both live in New York City. Yakie is here for the summer, like Gordo and me. They are super smart, and are studying to be a teacher.

"Yakie, have you seen all these plátanos? Abuela and I cut down el racimo a few days ago."

"Yes! ¡Hay muchos!"

"I want to make maduros, but we have to wait."

"Maduros are my papi's favorite. But do you know what my favorite way to eat a plátano is?"

"No, tell me!"

"Tostones!"

Before I know it, Yakie and I are peeling plátanos. We cut the plátanos into about seven pieces each. Then we fry them in a good amount of oil. When both sides are golden, Yakie places a piece in the hole of la tostonera.

I have to be careful because it's hot, hot, hot. I push down on the tostonera until the golden piece turns into a disk. That part always feels a little bit like magic.

Yakie carefully places the disks back to fry for a second time. The tostones float around in the pan like planets orbiting through space. Once they are even más dorados than before, it's time to take them out and lightly sprinkle them with salt.

Yakie likes to eat tostones dipped in mojo garlic sauce. I like to eat them with ketchup.

Abuela likes them with just some salt. And Gordo really doesn't care, as long as they've got a good crunch.

Later that evening, en el patio, Yakelin and I play dominó. I like to push the cool white tiles around on the wooden board. If I close my eyes, they sound like tiny thunderstorms. I collect my tiles in my hands. It's tricky to hold them all at once but, the bigger I get, the easier it is.

"Corazón, can I tell you something?"
"Yes, of course. ¿Qué pasó?"
"I have a surprise for Abuela."
"¡Dime, dime! Tell me! I won't spoil the surprise!"

Yakie whispers the surprise in my ear. My eyes light up like a full moon. Big and bright. Lightning bugs fly around in my chest. I am filled with excitement.

"How much longer?"
"Just one more week. El sábado."

Finally, Saturday! I run to the kitchen. Abuela is washing dishes at the sink while Yakelin sweeps the floor. I give both Abuela and Yakie besos on their cheeks. Yakie gives me a hug that says, "Today is the day. Hoy es el día."

I check on the plátanos. They are mostly black with some patches of yellow.

"Abuela, maduros tonight?"
Abuela glances over to the now small pile of plátanos. She looks back at me and says,

"Sí, Corazón. Maduros tonight."
Her voice is a mix of love and longing.

Around sunset, the sky is painted pink and purple. We hear a knock on the front door. Abuela goes to answer it.

She lets out un grito de felicidad.

"¡Ay, Dios mío! ¡Gracias a Dios, mi niño lindo! It's been so long!"

"Mamá, I've missed you so much!"

Their love, like a world with no borders.

I give my Tío Tomás un abrazo enorme. He smells like memories. Like togetherness and family.

That night we eat a mountain of maduros.

Tomorrow we will plant another plátano tree en nuestro patio.

Author Ro Peña (they/them) is a non-binary Afro-Caribbean Dominican from Washington Heights, New York City. Ro is passionate about science, nature, food, creativity, culture, and community. They are a lifelong learner and educator who centers their community building through identity affirmation surrounding gender, sexuality, race, ability, and emotional awareness. Ro has always had a deep love for children's literature and is eager to share their first story with you.

Illustrator Lillie DeLecuona (she/her) is a Cuban-American artist from Augusta, Georgia. She graduated with a BFA in Animation from the School of Visual Arts in New York City. When Lillie isn't making art, she is usually chasing around her four cats, reading comic books, or collecting jewelry (since she believes you are never truly dressed without a pair of funky earrings).

About Stirred Stories

The same stories have repeatedly been told.
We're here to stir that up.

We believe that in order to create a truly just society, the stories we consume must be diverse and equitable. That's why we center authenticity and diversity in everything we do, from the books we publish to how we publish them. In short, we're *publishing for a better tomorrow.*

Follow along with us at www.stirredstories.com.

Printed in the USA
CPSIA information can be obtained
at www.ICGtesting.com
LVHW060707161023
760421LV00007B/42